MONSTER MADNESS

THE STORY OF
THE LOCH NESS MONSTER

JENNIFER LOMBARDO

Enslow
PUBLISHING

Please visit our website, www.enslow.com. For a free color catalog of all our high-quality books, call toll free 1-800-398-2504 or fax 1-877-980-4454.

Library of Congress Cataloging-in-Publication Data
Names: Lombardo, Jennifer, author.
Title: The story of the Loch Ness monster / Jennifer Lombardo.
Description: New York : Enslow Publishing, 2023. | Series: Monster madness
   | Includes index.
Identifiers: LCCN 2021062170 | ISBN 9781978531789 (library binding) | ISBN
   9781978531765 (paperback) | ISBN 9781978531772 (set) | ISBN
   9781978531796 (ebook)
Subjects: LCSH: Loch Ness monster–Juvenile literature. |
   Monsters–Scotland–Juvenile literature.
Classification: LCC QL89.2.L6 L66 2023 | DDC 001.944–dc23/eng/20211222
LC record available at https://lccn.loc.gov/2021062170

Published in 2023 by
Enslow Publishing
29 E. 21st Street
New York, NY 10010

Copyright © 2023 Enslow Publishing

Designer: Tanya Dellaccio
Editor: Jennifer Lombardo

Photo credits: Cover YUCALORA/Shutterstock.com; p. 5 (Loch Ness) Susanne Pommer/Shutterstock.com; p. 5 (Loch Ness sign) Claudine Van Massenhove/Shutterstock.com; p. 7 Jan Holm/Shutterstock.com; p. 9 (two elephants) sukra13/Shutterstock.com; p. 9 (elephant swimming) Robert Fowler/Shutterstock.com; p. 11 (hippo), 21 (otter, cormorant) Eric Isselee/Shutterstock.com; p. 11 (hippo footprint) Karel Bartik/Shutterstock.com; p. 13 https://upload.wikimedia.org/wikipedia/commons/9/99/Loch_Ness_Monster-1.jpg; p. 15 (top) 3DF mediaStudio/Shutterstock.com; p. 15 (bottom) Gina Kelly/Alamy Images; p. 17 (illustration) Courtesy of Biodiversity Heritage Library/Flickr.com; p. 17 (skeleton) Lefteris Papaulakis/Shutterstock.com; p. 19 FedBul/Shutterstock.com; p. 21 (salmon) Boltenkoff/Shutterstock.com.

All rights reserved. No part of this book may be reproduced in any form without permission in writing from the publisher, except by a reviewer.

Printed in the United States of America

Some of the images in this book illustrate individuals who are models. The depictions do not imply actual situations or events.

CPSIA compliance information: Batch #CSENS23: For further information contact Enslow Publishing, New York, New York, at 1-800-398-2504.

CONTENTS

WHAT LIES BENEATH 4

AN OLD STORY 6

GROWING POPULARITY 8

LOOKING FOR FACTS 10

A FAMOUS PHOTO 12

AN ANCIENT CREATURE 14

WHAT IS IT? 18

GLOSSARY 22

FOR MORE INFORMATION 23

INDEX 24

Boldface words appear in the glossary.

WHAT LIES BENEATH

In Scotland, there are a lot of lochs—more than 30,000 of them, in fact! "Loch" is the Scottish word for a lake or sea **inlet**. Some of these lochs are said to be home to monsters. Stories of the Morag, which lives in Loch Morar, go back to at least 1902. A lake-horse has reportedly been spotted in Loch Arkaig.

Loch Ness has the largest volume of fresh water in Great Britain. Its monster, which is sometimes called Nessie, is the most famous of the loch monsters.

LOCH NESS IS ONE OF THE BIGGEST AND DEEPEST LAKES IN SCOTLAND.

Loch Ness

BELIEVE IT OR NOT!

LOCH NESS IS ALMOST 800 FEET (245 M) DEEP. IF YOU PUT THE EIFFEL TOWER IN THE LAKE, THREE-QUARTERS OF IT WOULD BE COVERED! IT'S THE SECOND-DEEPEST LAKE IN SCOTLAND. THE DEEPEST LAKE IS LOCH MORAR.

AN OLD STORY

Near Loch Ness, there's an ancient **Pictish** burial ground. In it, there are **carvings** of strange animals. Some people say the Picts knew about Nessie and made carvings of her. Others say the carvings are meant to be normal snakes.

The first written report of Nessie was made in 564 CE. Christians tell the story of Columba, an Irish man who later became a saint. When he was visiting Scotland, a monster came out of the loch and tried to attack someone. People said Columba stopped it with God's help.

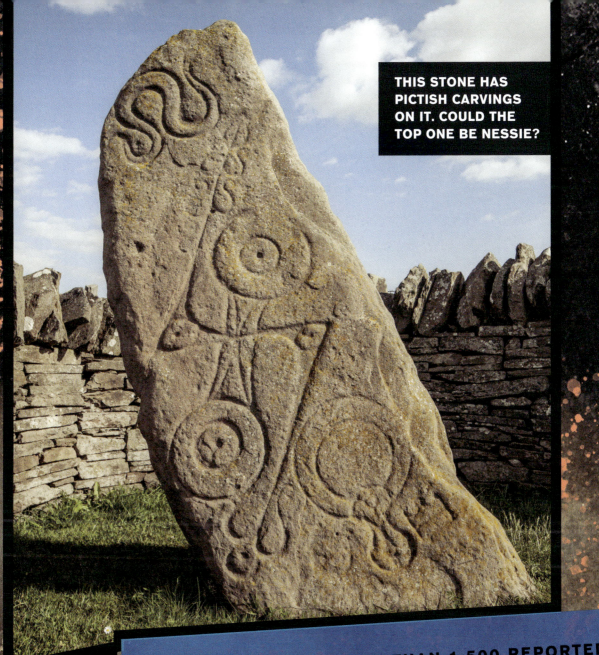

THIS STONE HAS PICTISH CARVINGS ON IT. COULD THE TOP ONE BE NESSIE?

BELIEVE IT OR NOT!

THERE HAVE BEEN MORE THAN 1,500 REPORTED NESSIE SIGHTINGS. THE MOST RECENT WAS IN 2021. A FLYING CAMERA CALLED A DRONE TOOK A PHOTO OF WHAT SEEMED TO BE A HUGE CREATURE SWIMMING IN THE LOCH.

GROWING POPULARITY

In 1933, a road was built on the shore of Loch Ness. People driving by could get a clear view of the loch for the first time. That year, a couple said they saw a huge animal swimming in the loch. They said it looked like a dragon or a dinosaur!

A local newspaper reported the story, and soon everyone was interested. A man named Bertram Mills offered £20,000 to anyone who caught Nessie for his circus. That's about $1.8 million today! However, some people think the circus owner knew he'd never have to pay anyone.

FROM FAR AWAY, A SWIMMING ELEPHANT COULD BE MISTAKEN FOR A CREATURE WITH A LONG NECK.

BELIEVE IT OR NOT!

IN 1933, MILLS'S CIRCUS WAS TRAVELING THROUGH SCOTLAND. SOME PEOPLE THINK THE FIRST MODERN NESSIE SIGHTING WAS ACTUALLY A SWIMMING ELEPHANT. THE COUPLE THAT DROVE QUICKLY PAST IN THEIR CAR MIGHT HAVE MISTAKEN THE TRUNK FOR A LONG NECK!

LOOKING FOR FACTS

After the first sighting, other people started saying they had seen Nessie, too. The *Daily Mail* newspaper hired a hunter named Marmaduke Wetherell to look for **evidence** that the monster existed. After a few days, he found huge footprints that he said were made by a four-legged animal. The *Daily Mail* reported that Nessie was real!

Wetherell made casts, or models, of the footprints by pouring **plaster** into them and waiting for it to dry. He sent the casts to the Natural History Museum in London, England.

HIPPO FOOTPRINTS ARE HUGE!

BELIEVE IT OR NOT!

THE MUSEUM WORKERS TOLD WETHERELL THE PRINTS CAME FROM A HIPPOPOTAMUS. EVERYONE AGREED THEY WERE LIKELY MADE BY A PERSON PLAYING A TRICK ON WETHERELL. THE *DAILY MAIL* REPORTED THE STORY AND MADE WETHERELL LOOK SILLY FOR BEING FOOLED.

A FAMOUS PHOTO

In 1934, R. Kenneth Wilson said he took a picture of the Loch Ness Monster. It became famous all over the world. Many people said it proved the Loch Ness Monster was real.

In 1994, Wetherell's stepson, Christopher Spurling, told the truth: The photo had been a trick! Spurling had made the "monster" by gluing a wooden model onto a toy **submarine**. Marmaduke Wetherell and his son, Ian, had taken the photo. Wilson agreed to give the photo to the paper so they wouldn't know Wetherell had anything to do with it.

BELIEVE IT OR NOT!

WETHERELL CAME UP WITH THE TRICK BECAUSE HE WANTED TO GET BACK AT THE *DAILY MAIL*. HOWEVER, MANY PEOPLE SAY THAT JUST BECAUSE THAT PICTURE WAS FAKE, IT DOESN'T MEAN THERE COULDN'T BE SOMETHING ELSE IN THE LOCH!

THIS FAMOUS PHOTO TURNED OUT TO BE FAKE.

AN ANCIENT CREATURE

Because of Wilson's photo, many people think Nessie could be a **plesiosaur**. Scientists say these animals died out about 66 million years ago. However, in 1938, scientists found a kind of fish called a coelacanth that they thought had died out around the same time.

Some people say finding the coelacanth shows that it isn't impossible for us to find a plesiosaur alive today. However, if there is a monster in Loch Ness, scientists say it's unlikely to be a plesiosaur. There are a few reasons for this.

THERE ARE TWO MAIN WAYS PEOPLE THINK NESSIE MIGHT LOOK.

BELIEVE IT OR NOT!

IN 2015, SCIENTISTS FOUND A COLD-BLOODED CREATURE THAT LIVED IN THE OCEAN NEAR SCOTLAND. IN 2020, THEY FOUND THE BONES OF A SMALL CREATURE THAT LOOKED LIKE A COMBINATION OF A PLESIOSAUR, AN ALLIGATOR, AND A T-REX. SOME PEOPLE THINK NESSIE MIGHT ALSO BE SOMETHING NEW.

One reason why Nessie might not be a plesiosaur is that this animal breathed air like dolphins and whales. They would have needed to come up for air a lot, so there would have been many more Loch Ness monster sightings by now if that were happening.

No plesiosaur could stay alive for millions of years, so if there is one in Loch Ness today, it would have to be the baby of past plesiosaurs. However, most people don't think there's ever been more than one Nessie. The loch doesn't have enough fish in it to keep even one plesiosaur fed for long!

BELIEVE IT OR NOT!

IN 2019, 18 PEOPLE REPORTED SEEING SOMETHING THAT MIGHT BE NESSIE. THIS IS THE HIGHEST NUMBER SINCE 1987. SOME OF THESE PEOPLE WERE VISITING THE LOCH. OTHERS SAW SOMETHING ON LOCH NESS'S 24-HOUR LIVE WEBCAM.

SHOWN HERE ARE THE BONES OF A PLESIOSAUR.

WHAT IS IT?

If Nessie isn't a plesiosaur, what is it? Scientists have been looking for answers for years. Some have used **sonar** to try to find out. A few times, the sonar has recorded large moving objects that scientists didn't recognize.

Scientists have also looked at the DNA of the creatures in Loch Ness. DNA is the part of the body that carries **genetic** information. In 2018, a team of scientists took samples of the water from many different parts of the loch. They looked at what DNA they found in the samples.

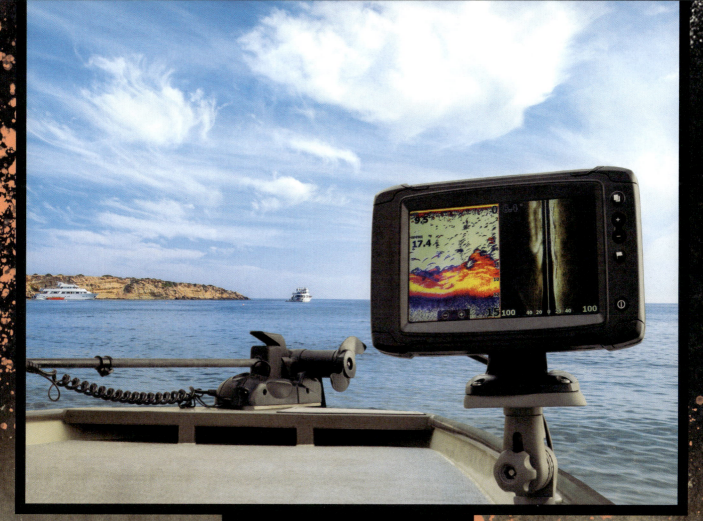

SONAR USES SOUND WAVES TO SHOW WHAT'S UNDERWATER.

BELIEVE IT OR NOT!

IN 1997, A TEAM OF SCIENTISTS PICKED UP AN OBJECT MOVING UNDERWATER ON THEIR SONAR. THEY SAID IT SEEMED LIKE A LIVING CREATURE. THE OBJECT WAS 15 FEET (4.5 M) LONG—THE SIZE OF A SMALL WHALE!

The DNA study found more than 3,000 kinds of animals in the loch! There were no large fish such as catfish or sharks. However, there was eel DNA in every sample. This makes scientists think Nessie might be a very large eel.

The DNA study isn't perfect, though. For example, people know for a fact that seals and otters sometimes visit the loch, but their DNA wasn't found by the scientists. Also, 20 percent of the DNA was unexplained. Maybe the Loch Ness monster's DNA is part of that!

BELIEVE IT OR NOT!

EELS CAN LIVE UP TO 100 YEARS, SO MODERN LOCH NESS MONSTER REPORTS COULD ALL BE THE SAME ANIMAL. HOWEVER, IF NESSIE IS ACTUALLY AN EEL, IT WOULDN'T BE THE ONE THE PICTS OR SAINT COLUMBA SAW.

ANIMALS FOUND IN LOCH NESS

FISH
SALMON
MINNOW
TROUT

BIRDS
HERON
DUCKS
CORMORANT

MAMMALS
SEALS
OTTERS

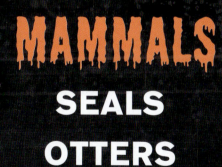

THIS CHART SHOWS SOME OF THE ANIMALS THAT ARE FOUND IN LOCH NESS'S WATERS.

GLOSSARY

carvings: Objects formed by cutting and shaping a material such as stone.

evidence: Something that helps show or disprove the truth of something.

genetic: Having to do with genes, or the parts of the body's cells that have to do with what a living thing looks like and how it grows.

inlet: A narrow area of water that goes into the land from a sea or lake.

Pictish: Having to do with the Picts, a group of people who lived in Scotland between the 3rd and 8th centuries.

plaster: A wet paste that hardens when it becomes dry.

plesiosaur: A meat-eating, water-dwelling reptile that died out with the dinosaurs.

sonar: A machine that uses sound waves to find things in a body of water.

submarine: A ship that can operate underwater.

FOR MORE INFORMATION

BOOKS

Gish, Ashley. *Loch Ness Monster*. Mankato, MN: Creative Paperbacks, 2020.

Pearson, Marie. *Loch Ness Monster*. Oxford, UK: Raintree, 2020.

Ransom, Candice F. *Mysterious Loch Ness Monster*. Minneapolis, MN: 2021.

WEBSITES

Dailymotion: "The Truth Behind the Loch Ness Monster"
www.dailymotion.com/video/xneo1m
In this show, experts try to figure out what Nessie really is.

Kiddle: "Loch Ness Monster Facts for Kids"
kids.kiddle.co/Loch_Ness_Monster
Learn more about Wetherell's photo trick and see pictures of models people have made of Nessie.

Worldcams: Loch Ness (Inverness) Webcam
worldcams.tv/united-kingdom/inverness/loch-ness
Search for Nessie yourself on this 24-hour live webcam.

Publisher's note to educators and parents: Our editors have carefully reviewed these websites to ensure that they are suitable for students. Many websites change frequently, however, and we cannot guarantee that a site's future contents will continue to meet our high standards of quality and educational value. Be advised that students should be closely supervised whenever they access the internet.

INDEX

Daily Mail, 10, 11, 13

DNA, 18, 20

eels, 20

elephants, 9

hippopotamus, 11

Loch Arkaig, 4

Loch Morar, 4, 5

otters, 20, 21

photos, 7, 12, 13, 14

Picts, 6, 7, 20

plesiosaur, 14, 15, 16, 17, 18

Saint Columba, 6, 20

sonar, 18, 19

Spurling, Christopher, 12

Wetherell, Ian, 12

Wetherell, Marmaduke, 10, 11, 12, 13

Wilson, R. Kenneth, 12, 14